KNITTING LANGUAGES

Stricken Knit Lavorare Tejer Strikke Tricoter Stick Prjóna 表

Cover design, David Xenakis
Back cover photo, Leah Trifanoff
Japanese graphics, Gayle Roehm

 Schoolhouse Press
6899 Cary Bluff
Pittsville, WI 54466

Library of Congress Catalog Card Number
96-69270

First Printing,1996

ISBN 0-942018-11-7

As well as publishing knitting books and producing
instructional knitting videos, *Schoolhouse Press*
offers a wide range of tools and materials for
handknitters. We will be pleased to send you a
catalogue upon request.

Knitting Languages

by

Margaret Heathman

Schoolhouse Press

DEDICATED

TO

Mary Maxine Conant

Table Of Contents

Introduction

Who would have thought it would take five years to compile a dictionary?

It began when I answered my telephone to find Meg Swansen on the other end. I had compiled a few pages of knitting terms for another project. Would I expand those languages, add some more, and have it published as a separate book? Having no clue of how to go about such a project, I agreed. Meg faxed me a cap pattern in several languages and wished me luck.

Soon after that I asked Bette and George Bornside if they knew any Swedish. "No, but we know a nun in Sweden who knits." So I headed for the post office for an Aerogram that was soon winging its way across the ocean to Sister Carol Burk in Sweden.

Sisters Carol Burk, Meryem Anna von Janson, and Gerda Breide sent me enough materials, patterns, and notes of historical knitting significance that I almost could write another book just on knitting in Sweden. What a tremendous resource! Sisters Meryem and Gerda even took the Danish section with them on their vacation to check my wording against the traditional knitting texts of Denmark.

In Sister Carol Burk's native New Orleans, I contacted Pastor Tryggve Andreassen of the Norwegian Seaman's Church. He was enthusiastic about my project and I left loaded down with magazines of knitting patterns, along with the name of a contact in the church's ladies' auxiliary.

After pleasant hours spent translating the Norwegian patterns, I contacted Inger Ryden of the NSC Ladies' Auxiliary. Inger enlisted the aid of Edith Godfray and Kari Vattøy, and the three delved into their heritage to give me the knowledge needed to represent the terms correctly.

iii

I also had the opportunity to cross-check a Norwegian anomaly with Linda Terry in Iowa and Arnhild Hillesland in Norway regarding the translation of the term "omgang" as it is used in "flat" knitting (see NOTES, page vii).

My Spanish and French "proofer" came in the form of a concierge at a small hotel in New Orleans. Francoise Moreno told me stories of growing up in France and Spain. In both places, the women of her family would gather regularly to knit and talk. It became my habit to sit and knit in the hotel's Atrium during my lunch breaks. Often Francoise would bring international knitters to visit with me, knitting being a universal language. Francoise eagerly agreed to reminisce her way through my list of Spanish and French terms.

Then came the trip to Italy. In Venice, I found Lella Bella Di Stella Elsa, a tiny knitters' shop I happened upon during one of the innumerable times I lost my way through that winding, twisting city of canals and bridges. What a wonderful time I had being lost that day! The small space was filled with yarn and Italian ladies chatting happily. That is, they were chatting until I came in, when they fell silent so the shopkeeper, who spoke no English, could attempt to assist me. With much gesturing and the aid of my list of Italian knitting terms, I carried on a laughter-filled conversation with all the ladies present. Finally, one customer stepped forward and proudly announced that she could speak some English. She said she had not come forward earlier because we were all having so much fun trying to communicate that she had not wanted to spoil our good time. All adventures in language should be so much fun!

Back in the U.S., I began making contacts regarding Japanese knitting terms. Lucinda Gresko and I had a long and productive discussion from our opposite coasts. Gayle Roehm helped me with the final editing and generously wrote the guidelines on page 81.

Christine Shaw, a professional race car mechanic and Electrical Engineer, came to my rescue with the German language. Together we covered her kitchen table with papers, ancient German texts, and dictionaries. After I thought we had covered everything, Chris told me some other references I needed to check. I know any errors in the German section are mine alone because she was incredibly persnickety and made sure each word or phrase was exactly right before allowing me to go on. Oh, that my own auto mechanic was that detail-oriented!

Icelandic - what a diverse language! Amy Beth Detjen in Minnesota, a buddy on the Internet's KnitList, sent me much-needed information that got me around the roadblocks I ran into while translating some patterns. I then contacted Dr. Marilyn van Keppel in Missouri and she agreed to look at my translated terms. I greatly appreciate the time she took from translating her own book of Faorese shawl patterns to assist me with this challenging language.

The final work you hold in your hands was possible only with the assistance of all of the persons mentioned above. Their knowledge helped me present the following translations so you can experience the true ethnicity of knitting in this wonderfully diverse world. My deepest gratitude to all those who assisted in bringing this book to life.

There is another group of people, much too large to name individually, who made sure this book became a reality. They are those friends, acquaintances, and co-workers who stood on the sidelines and cheered me on to completion (without even asking for a sweater in return). Thank you, thank you, thank you everyone!

♥ ♥ ♥

Notes

The Scandinavian languages of **Danish** and **Swedish** have "extra" letters in their alphabet. Notations at the beginning of each of those sections will direct you to specific letter locations.

There is no list of colors at the end of the **English/English** section. According to the British Consulate, colors (colours!) are the same for both the United States and Britain.

The **Japanese** section is the shortest and also does not include a list of colors. The Japanese system of charting and schematics is so explicit and detailed that words are practically redundant. Therefore, only the most often-used word symbols are included here. To work a design, just remember that Japanese patterns:

- Are always presented graphically
- Are usually shown in just one size
- Are measured in metric units
- Use graphs for stitch patterns

Icelandic has an alphabet containing unique letters. These have been arranged to fit with the English alphabet as closely as possible for ease in translating. When translating from the Icelandic, you will take mental leaps; that is, one word in Icelandic may replace an entire sentence in English.

Since **Norwegian** garments are knitted almost exclusively in the round, the following discussion of the word "omgang" (see page 90) is practically moot. However, you should be aware that there is some controversy over this word when it means "row" in *flat* knitting. Some Norwegians interpret it to mean knitting across one needle. Others interpret it as meaning to work across and back again -- in effect, working two rows. As there does not appear to be a firm definition regarding "omgang" as "row," you will need to consider the use of this word in the context of any *flat* knitted item. With regard to "omgang" as a "round", one round in Norway equals one round in the rest of the world.

Knitting in Danish

DANISH (DANSK) / ENGLISH

DANISH (DANSK)*	ENGLISH
Adskille	Separate
Adskilt	Separate
Aflukning	Casting off; binding off
Af gangen	Times
Afsluffe	Finishing
Alt	All
Altid	Always
Anbringe	To place
Andet steds	Patterns for which instructions are given separately
Antal	Number
Antal omgange	Number of rows
Antal omgange på længden	Number of rows in length
Arbejdet	Work (knitting)
Arbejdet vendes	To turn (the work)

* PLEASE NOTE: Danish words with a first vowel of "æ" or "ø" or "å" are listed at the end of each alphabetical section.

Knitting in Danish
Danish / English

Danish	English
Bag	Behind
Bag fra	Through back of loop
Bag masker op	Knit up stitches
Bagerste maskeled	Back loop (of st)
Begynde	Begin
Beskrivelsen gives separat	Patterns for which instructions are given separately
Blonde	Lace
Bomuld	Cotton
Bord	Border; front band
Brejt garnet	Break the yarn
Brystmål	Chest measurement
Bundt	Skein (hank)
Bytt(e)	Change
Bærestykket	Yoke
Bøj in	Fold in
Bånd	Stripe
Da	Then
De ulige (antal) pinde; hver anden = 2; tredje = 3	Odd number row

2

Del	Part
Dele i midten	Divide at the center
Den anden	Second
Den midterske maske	Central stitch
Derefter	Then
Derpå	Then
Dobbeltstangmaske	Double treble
Drejet	Into back of stitch; knit into back of stitch
Drejet maske	Twisted or crossed stitch
Efter	Follow
Eller	Or
Enhver	Every
En	One
En (1) løs af	Slip stitch
En maske løs af, strik to sammen træk den løse maske over; dobble indtagning	Slip one, knit two together, pass slipped stitch over (sk2togp)
En maske løs af	Slip a stitch
En ret en vrang	K1, p1 rib

Knitting in Danish
Danish / English

En størrelse	One size
Endre til	Change to
Enkel stangmaske	Treble
Enkell maske	Single crochet
Et sæt strømpepinde	Set of double-pointed needles
Farve	Color
Farvesammensætning	Color combination
Fastmaske	Single crochet; half double crochet
Fejl	Miss
Filsidel	Last
Flætning	Cable
Fold op	Hem
Forfra	Through front of loop
Forklaring	Explanation
Form	Shape
Forreste maskeled	Front loop of stitch
Forrige række	Previous row
Forstykket	Front

Først	First
Frå * til *	From * to *
Gange	Times
Garn	Yarn
Garnet brydes	Fasten off
Garnnøgle	Ball
Gentag	Repeat
Gentag mønster pinden	Repeat (as in pattern repeat)
Gentage disse X omgange	Repeat these X rows
Gentage fra * til *	Repeat from * to *
Glatstrikning	Plain knitting; stockinette stitch; stocking stitch
Gram	Grams
Gør modsat på (højre eller venstre side)	Reverse the instructions (right or left side)
Gøre	Make
Halsbånd	Collar
Halskant	Neckband
Halstørklæde	Scarf
Hele længden	Complete length

Hjælpepind	Cable needle; stitch holder
Hulmønster	Eyelet pattern
Hver	Each
Hver anden	Every other
Hæfte ende	Weaving
Hækle	Crochet
Hækle til bage	To work back (a stitch)
Hæklekant	Crochet border
Hæklet kant	Crochet border
Hæklenål	Crochet hook
Højre	Right hand
Højre forstykke	Right front
Højre pind	Right needle
Højrehånds	Right hand
Højreomslag	Yarn over needle before knit stitch
I alt	Altogether
I farve	In color
Igennem	Through

6

Indtagning	Decreasing
Jakke	Cardigan
Jævne omgange	Even number row
Kant	Border; edge
Kanten	Front borders
Kantmaske	Edge stitch
Knap	Button
Knaphul	Buttonhole
Knaphulskant	Front band
Knapper	Buttons
Knudekant	Beaded selvedge
Kort	Short
Krage	Collar
Krydse	To cross
Krydset maske	Cross stitch
Krydset retmaske	Through front of loop
Krydset vrangmaske	Through back of loop
Kun	Only
Kuppel	Cap

Knitting in Danish
Danish / English

Danish	English
Kæda	Chain (for crochet)
Kædemaske	Slip stitch
Lad stå de resterende masker	Leave remaining
Lade en maske falde	To drop a stitch
Lang	Long
Langdeniålet	Complete length
Langs med	Lengthwise
Lille	Small
Lomme	Pocket
Luffe af	To cast off or bind off
Luk af	Cast off
Luk af i mønstret	Cast off in pattern
Luk alle maskerne af	Cast off all stitches
Luk alle pindene af	Cast off all stitches
Lukke af for en maske	Stitch passed over
Læg garnet bag (om masken)	Yarn back
Læg garnet frem (for masken)	Yarn forward
Lægge	To place

Danish	English
Længde	Length
Længderibber	Rib
Lænkekant	Chain selvedge
Løkke	Loop
Manchet	Cuff
Maske	Stitch
Maske af	Bind off
Maske taget ret løs af	Slip stitch as if to knit
Maske taget vrang løs af	Slip stitch as if to purl
Maskeantallet deles med ... (example: 2 + 2 eller 6 + 2)	Work on a multiple of X plus X stitches
Maskeled af masken fra forrige række	Top of stitch (crochet)
Maskeholder	Stitch holder
Middel	Medium
Midte-; midti-; midten	Middle
Montering	To make up
Mønster	Pattern
Mønster (pinde)	Stitches used

Mønster som beskrives separat	Patterns for which instructions are given separately
Mønsteret	Repeat (as in pattern repeat)
Mål	Measurement
Måle	Measure
Nedre søm	Hem
Nummer	Number
Også	Also
Omgang	Round; row
Omgang (på 4 pinde)	Round (4 needles)
Omslag	Yarn around needle; yarn forward; yarn over
Op til ærmegabet	Body
Opskrift	Knitting pattern
Over hinanden	Over each other
Parlestrikning	Seed stitch
Passende	Suitable
Perlekant	Moss stitch edging
Perlestrikning	Moss stitch

Pinde	Needle
Placere	To place
Presse	Stretching
Pullover	Pullover sweater
På den højre	On the right
På den venstre	On the left
På samma måde	Alike; similarly
Resterarde	Remain
Retmaske	Knit plain (knit); knit stitch
Retpind	Knit row
Retsiden (af arbejdet)	Front or right side (of work)
Retstrikning	Knit plain; garter stitch
Retten	Right side
Rib	Rib
Ribkant	Rib
Ribmønster	Rib
Ribstikning	Ribbed knitting
Rullekrave	Turtle neck

11

Knitting in Danish
Danish / English

Rundpind	Circular needle
Rundstrikket strikketøj	Round knitting
Ryg	Back
Række	Round; row
Sam følger	Following
Samdidigt	At the same time
Saml (masker) op	To knit up or pick up (sts)
Saml maskerne op	Pick up stitches
Samle tabte masker op	To pick up dropped sts
Samme	Same
Side	Side
Sidekant	Selvedge
Silke	Silk
Skiftevis	Alternately
Skulder	Shoulder
Skuldersømmene	Shoulder seams
Skørt	Skirt
Slut af med	Last
Smal	Small

Som	As
Spring over	Skip over
Springe en maske over	Skip a stitch
Stangmaske	Double crochet; treble
Start	Beginning
Stor	Large
Stor ekstra	Extra large
Stor størrelse	Large sized
Straks	Then
Stribe	Stripe
Striber	Stripes
Stribet	Striped
Strik til arbejdet måler	Work even
Strik tilbage	Work back
Strikke	Knit; to knit
Strikke beskrivning	Knitting instructions; instruction
Strikke garnet sammen	Join
Strikke masker sammen	Together (sts)
Strikke op	To knit up or pick up (sts)

13

Knitting in Danish
Danish / English

Strikke ret	Garter stitch
Strikke rundl	Circular knitting
Strikke sammen	Knit together
Strikkefasthed	Gauge; tension
Strikkeopskrift	Knitting pattern
Strikkepind	Knitting needle; straight needle
Strikkes tilsvarende	Work as for
Strikketøj	Knitting
Sweater	Sweater
Sweater med rullekrave	Turtle neck sweater
Sy	Sew
Sy sømmene sammen	Sew seams
Sæt maskerne på ekstra pind	Place on stitch holder
Sæt på 4 strømpepinde	Set of double-pointed needles
Sætte	To place
Sætte maske på en hjælpepind	Leave sts on st holder
Sætte på ekstra pind	Leave remaining
Søm	Seam; hem

14

Sømkant	Seam edge
Størrelse	Size
Strømpepind	Double-pointed needles
Så	Then
Slå garnet om nålen	Take yarn around needle
Slå om	Yarn around needle; yarn forward; yarn over
Slå op	Cast on; casting on
Slå tråden om nålen inden ret masken	Yarn over needle before knit stitch
Slå tråden om nålen inden vrang masken	Yarn over needle before purl stitch
Tabe en maske	Drop a stitch
Tag en maske af, strik en, træk den løse maske over; enkel indtagning	Slip one, knit one, pass slipped stitch over (skp) or K2 together
Tag ind	Decrease
Tag op og strik	Pick up and knit
Tag op table masken	Pick up dropped sts
Tag ud	Increase
Tage ind	To decrease
Tage løs af	To slip

15

Tage maskelænkere op	To pick up loops or sts
Tage ud	To increase
Tilbageblivende	Remainder
To (2) ret to (2) vrang	K2, p2 rib
Total	Total
Trække en løkke	Draw through a loop
Trække en maske over	Stitch passed over
Trække garnet igennem en eller flere løkker	To draw through one or more loops
Tråd	Yarn
Tråden bagom	Yarn behind
Uden	Without
Udringningen	Neckline
Udtagning	Increase
Uld	Wool
Ulige antal masker	Odd number of stitches
Under	Under
Underarm	Underarm
Unse (= 28.4 grams)	Ounce
Vanstre forstykke	Left front

Vævet	Weaving
Venstre pind	Left needle
Venstreomslag	Yarn over needle before purl stitch
Vidde	Width
Vrang	Reverse stocking stitch
Vrangen	Reverse stocking stitch
Vrangen (af arbejdet)	Wrong side (of work)
Vrangmaske	Purl; purl stitch
Vrangpind	Purl row
Vrangsiden	Reverse stocking stitch
Vrangsiden (af arbejdet)	Wrong side (of work)
Være forsigtig	Take care
1 maske løs af, strikke 1 maske, træk den løse maske over	Slip one, knit one, pass slipped stitch over (skp) or K2 together
1 maske løs af, strikke 2 maske sammen, trække den løse maske over	Slip one, knit two together, pass slipped stitch over (sk2togp)
Ærme	Sleeve
Ærmegab	Armhole
Ærmekuppel	Sleeve cap shaping

Knitting in Danish
Danish / English

Åbent strikketøj (på 2 pinde)   Flat knitting (w/2 ndls)

Åbning   Opening

FARVE	**COLOR**
Blå(t)	Blue
Grøn; grønt	Green
Gul; gult	Yellow
Hvid(t)	White
Lyserød	Pink
Lys(t)	Light
Mørk(t)	Dark
Naturfarvet	Natural
Rosa	Pink
Rød; rødt	Red
Sort	Black
Ubleget; naturfarvet	Natural

Knitting in English

ENGLISH / ENGLISH
(United Kingdom / United States)

UNITED KINGDOM	UNITED STATES
Alternate	Every other
Balaclava	Cold weather hood; wimple
Cast off	Bind off
Double crochet	Single crochet
Double treble	Treble crochet
Grafting	Weaving
Half treble	Half double crochet
Hank	Skein
Jumper	Pullover sweater
Knit up	Pick up and knit
Make a stitch	Increase
Miss	Skip
Miss a stitch	Slip a stitch
Moss stitch	Seed stitch
Pick up loops	Pick up dropped stitches
Pick up stitches	Knit up stitches
Pins	Needles

Knitting in English
United Kingdom / United States

Polo neck	Turtle neck
Selvage	Edge
Slip stitch	Single crochet
Stocking stitch	Stockinette stitch
Tension	Gauge
Tension square	Gauge swatch
Top shaping	Cap shaping
Treble	Double crochet
Turtle neck	Mock turtle neck
Waist coat	Vest
Work straight	Work even
Yrn / Yon	Yo (Yarn over)

Knitting in French

FRENCH / ENGLISH

FRENCH	ENGLISH
Aiguille	Needle
Aiguille à tricoter	Knitting needle
Aiguille auxiliaire	Stitch holder or cable needle
Aiguille circulaire	Circular needle
Aiguille droite	Right needle
Aiguille gauche	Left needle
Alternativement	Alternate(ly)
Arrêter	Fasten off
Assembler	Join
A travers	Through
Augmenter	To increase
Augmentation	Increase
Avant	Before
Ayant	Having
Bandes des devant	Front bands
Bordures de devant	Front borders
Boucle	Loop

Knitting in French
French / English

Bouton(s)	Buttons
Boutonnier	Buttonhole
Bride simple	Treble- (Amer: Double) crochet
Bride double	Double treble (Amer: Treble)
Brin avant ou arrière	Back or front loop (of stitch)
Casser le fil	Break the yarn
Ce point s'execute avec un n. de m. div par X plus X m.	Work on a multiple of X plus X sts.
Chainette	Chain
Chaque	Each; every
Col	Collar
Comme	As
Commencant	Begin
Côté	Side
Côte	Rib
Côtes 1 x 1	K1, p1 rib
Côtes 2 x 2	K2, p2 rib
Coudre	Sew

Couler une ou plusieurs boucles	To draw through one or more loops
Couleur	Color
Couture	Seam
Crochet	Crochet or crochet hook
Croiser	To cross
De * à *	From * to *
Demi-bride	Half-treble (Amer: Half-double) crochet
Dernier (dern)	Last
Derrière (der)	Behind
Derrière (par)	Through back of loop
Dessous	Under
Dessous de bras	Underarm
Devant (dev)	Front
Devont droit	Right front
Devont gauche	Left front
Diminuer	To decrease
Diminution	Decrease
Dos	Back

Droite (à)	On the right
Echantillon	Tension
Emmanchure (emman)	Armhole
Empiecement	Yoke
En couleur	In color
Encolure	Neck
Endroit (de l'ouvrage)	Front or right side (of work)
Envers (de l'ouvrage)	Wrong side (of work)
Ensemble (mailles)	Together (stitches)
Epaules	Shoulders
Explications	Instructions
Faire	Make
Faire vis à vis	Reverse shapings
Fermenture des mailles	Cast off stitches; end of work
Fermer	Sew seams
Fermer en rond	Join into a ring
Fil	Yarn
Fil devant	Yarn forward

Fil derrière	Yarn back
Fois	Times
Former	Shape
Gauche (à)	On the left
Glisser	To slip
Grand	Large
Hauteur (ht)	Long; length
Hauteur totale	Complete length
Inversant les explications	Reverse the instructions
Jété a l'endroit	Yarn over needle before knit stitch
Jété a l'énvers	Yarn over needle before purl stitch
Jété (faire un jété)	Yarn forward, or yarn around the needle, or over
Jeter (le fil)	Take yarn round needle or hook
Jeu d'aigulles	Double-pointed needles
Jeu de 4 aigulles	Set of four double-pointed needles

27

Lâcher une maille	To drop one stitch
Laisser (lais)	Leave
Laisser en attente	Place on stitch holder
Lisière	Selvedge
Lisière chainette	Chain selvedge
Lisiere perlée	Beaded selvedge
Maille(s)	Stitch(es)
Maille central	Central stitch
Maille chainette	Chain
Maille coulée	Slip stitch
Maille croisée	Crossed stitch
Maille de tête	Top of stitch (crochet)
Maille en l'air	Chain
Maille endroit	Knit stitch
Maille envers	Purl stitch
Maille glissée endroit	Slip stitch as if to knit
Maille glissée envers	Slip stitch as if to purl
Maille impair	Odd number of stitches
Maille lisière	Selvedge stitch

Maille rabattue	Stitch passed over
Maille serrée	Double (Amer: Single) crochet
Maille torse	Twisted or crossed stitches
Manche	Sleeve
Mêmê	Same
Mêmê travail	Work as for
Milieu	Middle
Montage	Casting on
Monter	Cast on
Monter les mailles	Casting on
Moyenne	Medium
Nombre (nbre)	Number
Ourlet	Hem
Overture	Opening
Partager	Divide
Partager au milieu	Divide at the center
Partie	Part
Patron	Extra large

Pelotes (pel)	Balls
Petit	Small
Placer	To place
Poche(s)	Pocket(s)
Poignet	Cuff
Point	Stitch (pattern)
Point de boules	Bobble pattern
Point de chainette	Chain
Point de dentelle	Lace pattern
Point de riz	Moss stitch
Point fantaisie	Patterns for which the instructions are given separately
Point jersey endroit (end)	Stocking stitch
Point jersey envers (env)	Reverse stocking stitch
Point mousse	Garter stitch
Points employes	Stitches used
Première	First
Prendre	Change to
Puis	Then

Que le dos	The back
Quelque	Each; every
Rabattre (rab)	To cast off or to bind off
Rab comme les m. se presentent	Cast off in pattern
Rabattre les mailles	Finishing; cast off stitches
Rab pour l'epaule	Cast off for shoulder
Rab tout les m.	Cast off all stitches
Rang (rg)	Row
Rang impair	Odd number row
Rang pair	Even number row
Rang précédent	Previous row
1 rg end	Knit row
1 rg env	Purl row
Rattraper des mailles perdues	To pick up dropped stitches
Rayé	Striped
Rayures	Stripes
Relever	To knit up or pick up (stitches)

Remailler	To pick up the loops
Répéter	Repeat
Répéter tjrs ces X rgs	Repeat these X rows
Reprendre a	Repeat from
Restant(s)	Remaining
Revenir	To work back (a stitch)
Sans	Without
Sauter	Miss (a stitch) (Amer: skip a stitch)
Seconde	Second
Semblable	Alike
Separement (separem)	Separately
Simult	At the same time
Soin	Care
Sous	Under
Suivre (suiv)	Follow
Surjet simple	Slip one, knit one, pass slipped stitch over

Surjet double	Slip one, knit 2 together, pass slipped stitch over
Taille	Measurements
Temps	Times
Tension du travai fini	Stretching
Terminaison	Casting off or binding off
Tirer une boucle	Draw through a loop
Total	Total
Toujours (tjrs)	Always
Tour (4 aiguilles)	Round (4 needles)
Tour de poitrine	Chest measurement
Tourner l'ouvrage (travail)	To turn (the work)
Tous (ts)	All
Travail	Work
Tricot	Knitting
Tricoter	To knit
Tricoter a l'endroit	Knit plain (knit)
Tricoter a l'envers	Purl
Tricot à plat	Flat knitting

Knitting in French
French / English

Tricot en rond   Round knitting

Unique   One size

COULEUR	COLOR
Blanc	White
Bleu	Blue
Gris	Gray
Jaune	Yellow
Marron	Brown
Noir	Black
Orangé	Orange
Rose	Pink
Rouge	Red
Vert	Green
Violet	Purple

Knitting in German

GERMAN / ENGLISH

GERMAN	ENGLISH
Ab	From
Abheben	To slip
Abketten	To cast off; to bind off
Abketten der Maschen	Bind off stitches; cast off stitches
Abnehmen	Decrease
Abschrägen	Shape (of V-necks)
Ab*wiederholen	Repeat from *
Alle	All
Anfand der Reihe	Beginning of row
Anfang	Beginning
Anfangen	Begin
Anschlag	Casting on
Anschlagen	Cast on
Arbeit	Work
Arbeit einstellen	Fasten off
Arbeitsfolge	Knitting instructions
Arbeit wenden	To turn the work

Knitting in German
German / English

Armausschnitt	Armhole
Armel	Sleeve
Auf	On
Auffassen	To knit up or pick up (stitches)
Aufheben gefallener Maschen	To pick up dropped stitches
Aufnehmen	Increase
Aufschlag	Cuff
Aufwickeln	Unravel
Ausarbeiten	Making up
Ausarbeitung	Making up
Aussen	Outside
Baumwolle	Cotton
Beenden	Finishing
Bei	At
Beidseitig	Both sides; on each end (of row)
Bis	Until
Bleiben	Remain
Borte	Border; edging

Breite	Width
Dabei	At the same time; thereby
Dann	Then
Darüberstricken	Work (knit) across
Dauern	Last
Daron	Away; thereof; thereby
Der	The
Die Maschen wieder aufnehmen	To pick up the loops
Doppel	Double
Doppelstäbchen	Double-treble (Amer: treble) crochet
Durchziehen	Through
Ein doppelter Überzug (1 Ma abheben, 1 Ma abstricken und die abgehoben üder die gestrickte Masche ziehen)	Slip one, knit two together, pass slipped stitch over
Ein einfacher Überzug (1 Ma abheben, 1 Ma abstricken und die abgehobene über die gestrickte Masche ziehen)	Slip one, knit one, pass slipped stitch over
Eine Masche fallen lassen	To drop one stitch

39

Knitting in German
German / English

Ein Masche überziehen	Stitch passed over
Eine	One
Eine oder mehrere Schlingen abmaschen	To draw through one or more loops
Einmal	Once
Einsetzen	Insert
Ersten	First
Faden nach hinter Legen	Yarn back
Faden um die Nadel schlagen	Take yarn around needle or hook
Farbe	Color
Farben	Colors
Farbflächen	Area of color
Farbfolge	Color sequence
Farbwechsel	Color change
Fertigstellung	Binding off; casting off
Feste Masche	Double (Amer: single) crochet
Filz	Felting
Folgen	Follow
Folgt	Follow

Für	For
Ganze Länge	Total length
Garn	Yarn
Geeignet	Suitable
Gerade	Straight
Geschlossene Arbeit	Round knitting
Gestreift	Striped
Gestrickt	Knitted
Glatt links	Reverse stockinette stitch
Glatt rechts	Stockinette stitch
Glatt Maschen	Stockinette stitch
Gleich(e)	Alike; same
Gleich zeitig	At the same time
Gramm	Grams
Groß; grösse	Large
Grundmuster	Stitches used
Häkeln	Crochet
Häkelnadel	Crochet hook
Halbes Stäbchen	Half-treble (Amer: half-double) crochet

Knitting in German
German / English

Hals	Neck
Halsausschnit	Neck shaping; neck opening; neckline
Handschub	Glove
Hilfsnadel	Stitch holder or cable needle
Hinter	Behind
Hoch	High
Im Wechsel	Alternately
Immer	Always
In ähnlicher Weise	Similarly
Jede; Jeder	Each; every
Jedoch	Still
Kante	Edge; selvedge
Kettmasche	Slip stitch; chain
Kettenrand	Chain selvedge
Klein	Small
Knopf	Button
Knopfloch	Buttonhole
Kopfmasche	Top of stitch (crochet)

Kragen	Collar
Kraus gestricht	Garter stitch
Krause Masche	Purl stitch
Kreisumfang	Circumference
Kreuzen	To cross
Kurz	Short
Lang	Long
Länge	Length
Lassen	Leave
Linke Masche	Purl stitch
Linke nadel	Left needle
Links	Left; on the left
Locker	Loosely
Luftmasche; **Luftmaschenkette**	Chain
Mal	Times
Manschette	Cuffs
Masche	Stitch
Masche links abheben	Slip stitch as if to purl
Masche rechts abheben	Slip stitch as if to knit

Maschen	Stitches
Maschen ruhen lassen	Leave stitches on stitch holder
Maschenprobe	Tension
Maschenzahl teilbar durch	Stitches divisible by
Maß; Mass	Measurement; gauge
Mehrere schlingen Abmaschen	To draw through one or more loops
Mit	With
Mittel	Middle; center
Mittleren	Middle; center
Muster	Stitch pattern; pattern
Muster satz	Pattern repeat
Mütze	Cap
Nach	After
Nach hinten einstechen	In back of stitch; through the back loop
Nadel	Needle
Nähen	Sew
Naht	Seam
Nähte	Seams

Noch	Still; yet; in addition
Nur	Only
Oben	At the top
Obersten	Top
Oberweite	Actual chest measurement
Oder	Or
Offen	Open
Offene Arbeit	Flat knitting
Öffnung	Opening
Ohne	Without
Passend	Suitable
Perlrand	Beaded selvedge
Pullover mit Schildkrötkragen	Turtle neck sweater
Quaste	Tassle
Rand	Side; selvedge
Randmasche	Selvedge stitch
Rauhe Masche	Purl stitch
Recht glatte Masche	Knit stitch
Rechte Masche	Knit stitch

Knitting in German
German / English

Rechte Nadel	Right needle
Rechts	Right; on the right
Reihe	Row
Restliche	Remaining
Rock	Skirt
Rollkragen	Polo neck
Rückenteil	Back
Rückseite	Wrong side (of work)
Rückseite oben	Wrong side showing
Runde	Round; circular
Rundstricknadeln	Circular needle
Saum	Hem
Schal	Scarf
Schlichte Masche	Knit stitch
Schliessen	Close; sew up
Schlinge	Loop
Schlinge durchholen	Draw through a loop
Schulter	Shoulder
Schulter schrägung	Shoulder shaping

Schulterstück	Yoke
Seide	Silk
Seitenähte	Side seams
Seitennaht	Side seam
Sind	Are; there are
Spiel Stricknadeln	Double pointed needles
Spitze	Lace
Stäbchen	Treble (Amer: double) crochet
Streifen	Stripe
Stricken	To knit; knitting
Strickarbeit	Knitting
Strickjacke	Cardigan
Strickmuster	Stitches used
Stricknadel	Knitting needle
Strickschema	Diagram of pattern
Strickschrift	Of knitting pattern
Strümpfe	Socks
Tasche	Pocket
Teil	Part

German	English
Teilen	Parts
Über	Over
Übergehen	To skip (a stitch); to miss (a stitch)
Umfang	Circumference
Umhang	Shawl
Umlegen	Fold over
Umschlag fallen lassen	Drop the yarn over
Und	And
Unter	Under
Unterarm	Underarm
Unze	Ounce
Veränderung	Change
Verbinden	Join; unite
Verdrehte	Crossed; twisted
Verdrehte Masche	Twisted or crossed stitches
Verkreuzte Masche	Crossed stitch
Verschränke Masche	Twisted or crossed stitches
Verschränkt	Back of stitch
Verteilt	Distribute

Von	Of
Von hinten einstechen	Through back of loop
Vor	Before; in front of
Vorderes Maschenglied	Back or front loop (of stitch)
Vorderseite	Front or right side (of work)
Vorherig	Previous
Vorreihe	Previous row
Weben	Weave
Wechseln	Change; turn
Weiterarb	Continue to work
Weste	Vest
Wiederholungszeichen	Repeat from
Weite	Width
Weiterhin	From now on; continue to
Wenn	When
Wie	As
Wiederholen	Repeat
Wolle	Wool
Zahl	Number

Knitting in German
German / English

Zur runde schließen	Join into a ring
Zurückstricken	To work back (a stitch)
Zusammen	Together
Zwei	Two
Zweimal	Twice
Zweite	Second
1 Umschlag	Yarn forward; yarn around needle; yarn over
1M re, 1M li	K1, p1 ribbing
2M re, 2M li	K2, p2 ribbing

FARBE	**COLOR**
Blau	Blue
Braun	Brown
Dunkel	Dark
Gelb	Yellow
Grau	Gray
Grün	Green
Hell	Light
Lila	Lilac; purple
Rosa	Pink; rose
Rot	Red
Schwarz	Black
Weiß	White

Knitting in Icelandic

ICELANDIC / ENGLISH

ICELANDIC	ENGLISH
Á eftir	Behind
Á líkan hátt	Similarly
Affelling	Cast(ing) off/bind(ing) off
Afgangur	Remainder
Allir; allur	All
Allt af	Always
Alveg; algjörlega	Altogether
Annar	Second
Annast um	Care of (woolen articles); take care of
Augnprjón	Lace knitting
Auka	Increase
Auka stór	Extra large
Aukið i með að bregða um prjón	Yarn around needle
Aukið i med að prjóna tvisvar i sömu lykkju, fyrst framan i siðan aftan i	Increase by knitting both sides of a stitch

Knitting in Icelandic
Icelandic / English

Aukið i med að snúa upp á bandið milli lykkja	Increase by picking up the right side of the stitch from the previous row
Aukið i með að snúa upp á bandið milli lykkja	Make one (increase)
Baðmull	Cotton
Bageste maskelæmke	Back loop (of st)
Bageste maskelænke	Back of stitch
Bak	Back
Bakvið	Behind
Begge maskelænker	Both sides of stitch
Bómullargarn	Cotton yarn
Borði	Edging
Brjóststykki	Front
Brúgðið um prjóninn	Yarn over
Brugðin lykkja	Purl stitch
Brugðin lykkja skekkt	Twisted purl stitch
Brugðning	Purl
Brydding	Edging
Byrja	Begin
Byrjun	Beginning

Eða	Or
Eftir lengdinni	Lengthwise
Eftirfarandi	Following
Eftirstöðvar	Remainder
Einn	Only
Einnig	Also
Eins; jafnt	Alike
Eins; svo	As
Endurtekning	Repeat (as in pattern repeat)
Ermar	Sleeve
Ermilengd	Sleeve length
Faldur	Hem
Fastahekl; uppfitjun með föstum lykkjum	Double crochet
Fella niðr lukkju	Drop a stitch
Flóki; flókahattur	Boiled wool (felting)
Flykingarbrjóst	Front
Forreste maskelænkle	Front loop (of st); front of stitch
Frá * að *	From * to *

Knitting in Icelandic
Icelandic / English

Frágangur	Finishing
(Frakka) laf; pils; jaðar; rönd; útskækill	Skirt
Framhlið	Front; front band
Fylgja; fara (komo) á eftir	Follow
Fyrir utan	Without
Fyrstur	First
Gangar í krákustig eða hvössum bugðum	Zigzag movement
Garðaprjón	Garter stitch
Garn	Yarn
Gataprjón	Lace knitting
Gera; búa til; smíða	Make
Hálsband	Neckband
Handvegur	Armhole
Hanzki; glófi; fingravetlingur	Glove
Hekla; hekl	Crochet
Hekluð upp lykkja	Pick up (dropped sts)
Heklunálar	Crochet hook
Hnappagat	Buttonhole

Hnappur	Button
Hneppa	Buttons
Hnöttur; kúla; bolti	Ball
Hnýta; prjóna	Knit
Holmál	Gauge
Hoppa	Skip (a stitch)
Hringprjónn	Circular needle(s)
Hryggur	Back
Húfa; hvellhetta	Cap
Húsgangsfit	Casting on with 2 ends
Hvert ár	Every other
Hvor (hver)	Each
Hæfilegur; hentugar; vel til fallinn	Suitable
Hægri	Right (as opposed to wrong)
I bageste maskelænke	Into back of stitch
I gegnum; yfir; fyrir	Through
Jaðar	Selvedge
Jaðarlykkja	Selvedge stitch
Kaðlaprjón	Cable stitch

Keðjulykkjur	Single crochet
Kensla; fræðsla; fyrirsögn	Instruction
Kragi; hálslín; hálsband; hálshringur	Collar
Langur; langorður	Long
Lárjettur	Horizontal
Lengd; lengja	Length
Líka	Also
Lítið auga	Eyelet pattern
Litur	Color
Loðrjettur	Vertical
Loftlykkjur	Chain (for crochet)
Lykkja	Stitch
Lykkja; hanki; hnezla	Loop
Lykkju-fall	Drop a loop so as to leave a hole
Lykkjujaðar	Chain selvedge stitch
Mansjetta; högg; uppslag (á ermi)	Cuff
Með vopnum	Underarm

Miðja; miðbik; meðaltal; meðalstig	Medium
Miður; mið-; meðal-	Middle
Minka	Decrease
Munstureining	Pattern
Mynda; laga; sniða	Shape
Mæla; mælast	Measure
Mæling	Measurement
Nál	Needle
Næstur	Second
Og	And
Ok	Yoke
Op; gat; byrjun	Opening
Overtraæknings indtagning	Bind off
Öxl; axla	Shoulder
Partur; hluti	Part
Þá	Then
Perluprjón	Moss stitch; seed stitch
Peysubolurinn	Body of a garment
Peysuprjónar; bandprjónn	Knitting needle

Knitting in Icelandic
Icelandic / English

Peysuprjónar	Straight needles
Þrengja (kreppa) að; þrýsta á	Press
Þrihyrndur geiri í fati; spjald í skyrtu	Gusset (underarm)
Prjonafesta	Gauge
Prjónaðar 2 lykkjur saman brugðnar	Purl two sts together
Prjónaðar 2 lykkjur saman slétt	Knit two sts together
Prjónaðferð	Pattern
Prjónaskapur	Knitting
Þunnur	Thin yarn
Þykkur	Thick yarn
Rekja upp	Unravel
Rjetthverfan	Right (as opposed to left)
Rönd; brydda; landamæri	Border
Rönd; egg	Edge
Rönd	Stripe
Röndó hur	Striped
Rúllukantur	Rolled edge

Saman	Together (sts)
Samskeyti	Scarf
Samtals	Total
Samur	Same
Sauma	Sew
Sauma saman	Sew together
Saumur	Seam
Siða	Side
Silki	Silk
Sinnum	Times
Sjal	Shawl
Sjerhver; hver; allir	Every
Skilja; aðskilinn; sjerstakur	Separate
Skólafit	Casting on
Skúfur	Tassle
Skýring; útlistun	Explanation
Slétt lykkja	Knit stitch
Slétt lykkja steypt yfir 2 sléttar samman	Slip one, knit two together pass slipped stitch over (sk2togp)

Knitting in Icelandic
Icelandic / English

Slétt prjón	Stockinette or stocking stitch
Sljetta	Iron
Smár; litill	Small
Snarhlykkjóttur	Zigzag
Snúa(e-u) við; breyta algjörlega; umsteypa	Reverse
Snúin, slétt lykkja	Twisted knit stitch
Snúningur	Rib; ribbed knitting
Snúningur 1 slétt 1 brugðin	K1, p1 rib
Snúningur 2 sléttar 2 brugðnar	K2, p2 rib
Sokkaprjónar	Set of (5) double-pointed needles
Steyplúrtaka	Decreasing sts by binding/casting off
Stígvjelatrje; skókeustu	Last
Stór	Large
Stuttur; skammur; lágur	Short
Stærð	Size
Söma tegundar; alveg eins	In one piece
Taka upp lykkju	Pick up stitches

Tala; fjöldi; númer	Number
Tekin óprjónuð fram af brugðin	Slip stitch as if to purl
Tekin óprjónuð fram af slétt	Slip stitch as if to knit
Tengja (skeyta); saman	Join
Til skiftis; á víxl	Alternately
Tvöfáldur stuðull	Double treble
Ull	Wool (in its natural state)
Ullargarn; gróft	Wool yarn (4-ply thick)
Umferð	Row
Umferðir	Rows
Undanfarandi	Previous
Undir; fyrir neðan	Under
Uppfitjun með stuðlum	Treble crochet
Vasi	Pocket
Vefa; fljetta saman	Weave
Vera efter	Remain
Verða af; missa (e-s)	Miss
Verfæraskrín; fiskakarfa	Kit

Verk; vinna	Work (knitting)
Vesti	Vest
Viða; vinda; hönk	Skein (hank)
Vidd; breidd	Width
Yfirvídd	Circumference
2 lóð (half an ounce = lóð)	Ounce

LITUR	COLOR
Apelsína	Orange
Blár	Blue
Buúnn	Brown
Dimmur	Dark
Grænn	Green
Grár	Grey
Gulur	Yellow
Hvitur	White
Ljettur	Light
Mórautt	Reddish brown
Náttúrlegur; bleikr	Natural
Nellika; ljósrauður	Pink
Purpuri	Purple
Rauður	Red
Svartur	Black

Knitting in Italian

ITALIAN / ENGLISH

ITALIAN	**ENGLISH**
Accavallare	Pass; slip
Accavallato	Slip 1, knit 1, pass slipped stitch over
Accavallato doppia	Slip 1, knit 2 together, pass slipped stitch over
Alternativamente	Alternately
Alternatamente	Alternately
Altezza	Length
Altezza totale	Total length
Altri	Another
Ancora	Again; more
Apertura	Opening
Asola	Loop
Assieme	Together
Attaccare	Sew; attach
Attesa (lasciare le maglie in attesa)	Leave stitches on stitch holder
Attraverso	Through
Aumentare	To increase

67

Aumenti	Increases
Aumento	Increase
Avviare	Cast on
Bordino	Border
Bordo	Border
Bottone	Button
Cambiare	Change
Campione	Tension
Cappuccio	Hood
Catenella	Chain
Centrale	Central;center
Chiudere	Cast off
Chiudere in tondo	Join into a ring
Colletto	Collar
Collo	Collar
Colore	Color
Con il filo dav	With yarn in front
Con il filo dietro	With yarn in back
Confezione	Casting on; making up

Contemporaneament	At the same time
Continuare	Continue
Coste 1 X 1	Knit 1, purl 1 ribbing
Coste 2 X 2	Knit 2, purl 2 ribbing
Cucitura	Seam
Davanti	Front
Destra	On the right
Dietro	Back; through back of loop
Diminuire	To decrease
Diminuzione	Decrease
Diritto	Knit stitch
Diritto del lavoro	Front or right side of work
Disegno	Diagram
Dispari	Odd number (of rows)
Distribuendo nel corso del ferro	Spacing evenly across the row
Doppio	Double; twice
Due	Two
Esecuzione	Instructions

Eseguire	Make; work
Estrarre un asolo	Draw through a loop
Far cadere una maglia	To drop a stitch
Fermare	Fasten off
Ferri	Rows; needles
Ferro	Row; needle
Ferro ausiliario	Stitch holder or cable needle
Ferro circolare	Circular needle
Ferro de calza	Knitting needle
Ferro destro	Right needle
Ferro sinistro	Left needle
Filati	Yarn
Filo	Yarn
Filo davanti	Front loop (of stitch)
Filo dietro	Back loop (of stitch)
Foretti	Holes; slots for ribbon
Frangia	Fringe
Gettare (il filo)	Take yarn around needle or hook

Gettato (fare un)	Yarn forward; yarn around the needle; yarn over
Gettato	Yarn over needle; yarn around needle; yarn forward
Gioco de ferri	Set of double-pointed needles
Giro	Round (on four needles)
Girocollo	Round or crew neck
In senso inverso	Reverse shaping
Incavo manica	Armhole
Incrociare	To cross
Iniziare	Begin
Insieme	Together
Intrecciare	Bind off; cast off
Intrecciare a costa	Bind off in rib
Lato	Edge; side
Lavorare in tondo	Work in rounds
Lavoro in tondo	Round knitting
Lavorare a maglia	To knit

Knitting in Italian
Italian / English

Lavorare su un numero de m. multiplo de X plus X	Worked on a multiple of X plus X stitches
Lavoro	Work
Lavoro a maglia	Knitting
Lavoro a piatto	Flat knitting
Lunghezza	Length
Maglia	Stitch
Maglia accavallata	Stitch passed over
Maglia catenella	Chain
Maglia de testa	Top of stitch (crochet)
Maglia diritta	Knit stitch
Maglia dir ritorto	Knit through back of loop
Maglia doppio	Knit into next stitch one row below
Maglia incrociata	Crossed stitch
Maglia passata a dir	Slip stitch as if to knit
Maglia passata a rov	Slip stitch as if to purl
Maglia rasata	Stockinette stitch
Maglia rasata rovescia	Reverse stockinette stitch

Maglia ritorta	Twisted or crossed stitches
Maglia rovescia	Purl stitch
Maglia rovescia ritorto	Purl through back of loop
Maglia vivagno	Selvedge stitch
Maglia volante	Chain
A metá	In half
Mezzo punto alto	Half-treble (Amer: half-double) crochet
Misure	Measurements
Morbidamente	Loosely
Nello stesso modo	In the same way
Occhielli	Buttonholes
Occorrente	Materials
Ogni	Each; every
Orlo	Hem
Pari	Even number of rows
Passare	To slip
Passare una o più	To draw through one or more loops
Passare 1 dir senza lavorarlo	Slip one as if to knit

73

Passare 1 rov senza lavorarlo	Slip one as if to purl
Per	Through; for
Piegare	Turn; fold
Più	More
Proseguire	Continue
Punti divisi da	Stitches divisible by
Punti impiegati	Stitches used
Punto	Stitch
Punto alto	Treble (Amer: Double) crochet
Punto alto doppio	Double-treble (Amer: treble) crochet
Punto basso	Double (Amer: single) crochet
Punto fantasia	Patterns for which the instructions are given separately
Punto a grano di riso	Moss stitch
Punto legaccio	Garter stitch
Punto passato	Slip stitch
Punto scivolato a dir	Slip one as if to knit
Punto scivolato a rov	Slip one as if to purl

Quando	When
Quindi	Then
Raglan	Raglan
Regolarmente	Evenly
Rimanente	Remaining
Rimasto	Remaining
Rip il disegno	Repeat the pattern
Ripetere da * a *	Repeat from * to *
Riprend	Pick up
Riprendere	Pick up
Rovescio	Purl stitch
Rovescio (del lavoro)	Wrong side (of work)
Sbieco	Slope; shaping
Scalfo manica	Armhole
Scollo	Neck
Scollo a V	V-neck
Sequito	Following
Sinistra	On the left
Sotto	Under

Knitting in Italian
Italian / English

Spalle	Shoulders
Sparse	Evenly distributed
Spiegazione	Instructions
Successivo	Following
Sul diritto del lavore	On right side of the work
Sul roviescio del lavore	On wrong side of the work
Taglia	Size
Tenere in attesa	Leave unworked
Terminare	End
Traforato	Lacy
Treccia	Cable
Uguale	Alike
Ultimo	Last
Uncinetto	Crochet or crochet hook
Vivagno	Selvedge stitch
Vivagno a catenella	Chain selvedge
Vivagnbo perlato	Beaded selvedge
Voltare il lavoro	To turn (the work)
(Una) volta	Once

Volte	Times
2 m. ins a dir	Knit two together
2 m. ins a rov	Purl two together

Knitting in Italian
Italian / English

COLORE

Arancionne   Orange

Azzurro   Blue

Bianco   White

Giallo   Yellow

Grigio   Gray

Marrone   Brown

Nero   Black

Rosa   Pink

Rosso   Red

Verde   Green

Viola   Purple

Vivace   Bright

COLOR

78

Knitting in Japanese

JAPANESE / ENGLISH

JAPANESE	**ENGLISH**
後	Back
ボタン穴	Buttonhole
作	Cast on; make
衿	Collar; neckband
減	Decrease
前	Front
ゲージ	Gauge
増	Increase
表	Knit or front (refers to the front side of the stitch)
号	Needle size

Knitting in Japanese
Japanese / English

模 様	Pattern
裏	Purl or back (refers to the back side of the stitch)
段	Row
袖	Sleeve
目	Stitch
メリヤス	Stockinette stitch
編	To knit
糸	Yarn
かけ目	Yarn over

Although the above terms may be helpful, you may find that you do not need them often. Japanese knitting patterns are always presented graphically. A pattern consists of three major sections: (1) some introductory material, such as yarn requirements, sequence of working and comments on the style; (2) schematics for each garment part; and, (3) stitch charts, which always show the stitch patterns as symbols.

With a little patience, you can knit from the schematics and stitch charts by determining which numbers on the schematics refer to stitches/rows (followed by *me* or *dan*) and which refer to garment measurements (usually followed by "c" or "cm").

You should also be aware of these characteristics of Japanese patterns:

• The patterns are shown in only one size. Look at all measurements and adjust for your own proportions.

• Measurements are always given in centimeters.

• Pay attention to the direction of the knitting, indicated by an arrow on the schematic. Frequently, ribbing is added last. Shaping, such as an armhole, is always shown in the direction of the knitting, and is always given as rows/stitches/times.

• Japanese needle sizes differ from American and metric, so always swatch.

81

Knitting in Norwegian

NORWEGIAN / ENGLISH

NORWEGIAN	**ENGLISH**
All	All
Alltid	Always
Alt	All
Andre	Second
Annenhver	Alternately
Antall masker	Number of stitches
Arbeid	Work
Attersting	Backstitch
Avslutning	Finishing
Åpning	Opening
Bak	Behind
Bakenfor	Behind
Bakfra	Back loop (of st)
Bakstykke	Back
Bare	Only
Begynn på nytt	Start over
Begynne	Begin
Begynnelse	Beginning

Behandle	Take care of
Behandling av (ulltøy)	Care of (woolen articles)
Blonde	Lace
Boble mønster	Bobble pattern
Bole	Body
Bomull	Cotton
Bord	Border
Brett inn	Fold in
Brystvidde	Chest measurement
Bærestykke	Yoke
Da	As; then
De bakerste	Last
De siste	Last
Dele	Divide
Dele på midten	Divide at the center
Del	Part
Det som er igjen	Remainder
Diagram	Chart
Dusk	Pompom; tassle

Ekstra stor	Extra large
Eller	Or
En som strikker	Knitter
En størrelse	One size
Erme	Sleeve
Ermehol	Armhole
Ermhull	Armhole
Et par vanter	A pair of gloves
Etter	After
Fall	Hem
Farge	Color
Fargesammensetning	Color combination
Fell(e) av alle masker	Cast off all stitches
Fell(e) av i mønster	Cast off in pattern
Felle	Decrease
Felle av	Bind off; cast off
Felle et antall masker	Decrease a number of sts
Felling	Binding or casting off; decreasing
Feste	Fasten off

85

Flette	Cable
Fordele på 4 pinner	Distribute on four needles
Foregående	Previous
Foregående omgang	Previous row
Forklaring	Explanation
Forkortelser	Abbreviations
Forme	Shape
Forming av tommel (i votter)	Thumb shaping (in mittens)
Fortsette	Continue
Forside	Front or right side of work
Forstykke	Front
Fra * til *	From * to *
Følge etter	Follow
Følgende	Following
Først	First
Ganger	Times
Garn	Yarn
Genser	Pullover sweater; sweater
Gjennom	Through

Gjenta	Repeat (as in pattern repeat); to repeat
Gjenta disse X omganger	Repeat these X rows
Gjenta fra * til *	Repeat from * to *
Gjentatte	Repeated
Glassperle	Bead
Glattstrikking	Stockinette stitch
Gram	Grams
Hals	Neck binding (crew neck or V-neck)
Halslinning	Neckband
Halsringning	Neck shaping
Halsutringning	Neckline
Hekle	Crochet
Heklekant	Crochet border
Heklenål	Crochet hook
Hel lengde	Complete length
Hempe	Loop
Hespel	Skein (hank)
Hjelpepinne	Cable needle

Hold maskene på maskeholder	Leave sts on st holder
Holde igjen de resterende	Leave remaining
Holde maskene på hjelpepinne	Leave sts on cable needle
Hopp over (en maske)	Skip (a stitch)
Hoppe	Skip
Horisontal	Horizontal
Hull	Opening; hole
Hullrad	Eyelet pattern
Hver	Each; every
Hver annen	Every other
Hver for seg	Separately
Høyhalset genser	Turtle neck sweater
Høyre	Right (as opposed to left)
Høyre forstykke	Right front
Høyre hånd	Right hand
Høyre pinne	Right needle
Høyre side	Right side (of work - as opposed to the left side of the work)

I alt	Altogether
I ett stykke	In one piece
I farge	In color
I forkant av masken	Front loop (of st)
Igjennom	Through
Instrukser; instruksjoner	Instructions
Jakke	Cardigan
Jare	Selvedge
Jevnt fordelt	Evenly spaced
Kant	Edge; selvedge
Kantmaske	Edge stitch; selvedge stitch
Kast på pinne	Take yarn around needle
Kast på pinnen	Yarn around needle; yarn forward; yarn over
Kile	Gusset (underarm)
Klipp(e) av garnet	Break the yarn
Knapp	Button
Knapper	Buttons
Knappestolpe	Buttonband
Knapphull	Buttonhole

Knapphullstolpe	Buttonhole band
Knyt en knute	Tie a knot
Kontrastfarge (ikke brukt i mønsteret, men som foreløpig maskeholder som senere skal fjernes, for eks. til tommel i votter eller lommer)	Contrasting color (not used in pattern, but as a temporary stitch holding yarn to be later removed, such as for thumb in mittens or for pocket opening)
Kors	Cross
Korssting	Cross stitch (embroidery)
Kort	Short
Krage	Collar
Krysse	Cross; cross a stitch
Lage	Make
Lang	Long
Langsetter; langsmed	Lengthwise
Legge ut	Increase
Legge opp	Cast on
Lengde	Length
Likt antall pinner	Even number row
Liten	Small

Loddrett	Vertical
Lomme	Pocket
Lue	Cap
Luftmasker	Slip stitch
Løkke	Loop
Mansjett(er)	Cuff(s)
Maske	Stitch
Maskenål	Stitch holder
Mellom-	Middle
Middels	Medium
Midt -	Middle
Midten	The middle
Midtmaske	Central stitch
Minske	Decrease
Miste en maske	Drop a stitch (accidentally)
Montere	Assemble
Montering	To put together
Mål	Measurement
Måle	Measure

Mønster	Pattern
Mønster maske	Pattern stitch
Mønsterpakke med garn	Kit
Neste pinne	Following row
Nummer	Number
Nøste	Ball
Også	Also
***Omgang**	Round; row
Opplegg	Casting on
Oppskrift	Knitting pattern
Oppslag (på erme)	Cuff(s)
Over	Over
Over hverandre	Over each other
Øke	To increase
Økning for erm	Increase for sleeve shaping
Passende	Suitable
Perlebrodert	Beaded
Perlestrikk	Moss or seed pattern

* See NOTES, page vii, for explanation of definition.

Pinne(r)	Needle(s); straight knitting needles
Pinne nummer	Needle size
Plukk opp	Pick up
Plukk opp masker	Knit up stitches
Plukk opp og strikk rett	Pick up and knit
Presse	Iron; press
På samme måte	Alike; similarly
På samme tid	At the same time
Prøve	Swatch (for gauge)
Redusere	Decrease
Rekke opp	Unravel
Rett; riktig	Right (as opposed to wrong)
Rette	Front or right side of work
Rettmaske	Garter stitch
Rettside	Right side (of work-the side that shows)
Rundpinne	Circular needle
Rundstrikk	Round knitting
Rundstrikning	Circular knitting

Ryggen	The back
Samlet	Total
Samme	Same
Sammen	Together (sts)
Sammentagning	Decreasing (knit together)
Samtidig	At the same time
Separat	Separate
Sett på maskeholder	Place on stitch holder
Sette	Place
Side	Side
Silke	Silk
Siksak	Zigzag
Sjal	Shawl
Sjal farge	Shawl color
Skift(e) til	Change to
Skifte	Change
Skjerf	Scarf
Skjørt	Skirt
Skulder	Shoulder

Skuldersømmer	Shoulder seams
Slippe	To drop a stitch
Sløyfe	Miss; omit
Snu (arbeidet)	To turn (the work)
Som	As
Spenne	Stretch (how much a knitted fabric does)
Springe over	Skip
Stolpe	Front band
Stor	Large
Stor størrelse	Large size
Størrelse	Size
Strekke	Stretch (how much a knitted fabric does)
Strekke i fasong	Stretch (the pieces for blocking)
Strikke	Knit
Strikke oppskrift	Knitting patterns
Strikke maske	Knit stitch
Strikke pinne	Knit row
Strikke fasthet	Gauge

Strikke rett	Knit plain (knit)
Strikke sammen	Knit together
Strikke vridd rett	Into back of stitch; knit into back of stitch; through back of loop
Strikkefasthet	Tension
Strikkepinne	Knitting needle;straight needle
Strikketøy	Knitting
Stripe	Stripe
Striper	Stripes
Stripet	Striped
Stryke	Iron; press
Strømpepinne(r)	Double-pointed needle(s)
Strømpepinner	(Set of) double-pointed needles
Sy	Sew
Sy sammen	Sew together; join
Sy sømmer	Sew seams
Så	Then
Søm	Seam

Søm kant	Seam edge
Sømrom	Seam allowance
Ta en maske løs av	Slip a stitch
Ta løs av	Slip
Ta opp masker	Pick up stitches
Ta rett av	Slip stitch as if to knit
Ta vrang av	Slip stitch as if to purl
Ta 1 m løs av, 1 r, trekk den løse m over	Slip one, knit one, pass slipped stitch over (skp)
Ta 1 m løs av, 2 r sm, trekk den løse m over	Slip one, knit two together pass slipped stitch over (sk2togp)
Til høyre	On the right
Til venstre	On the left
Trekke igjennom løkken	Draw through the loop
Tykt garn	Thick yarn
Tynt garn	Thin yarn
Ulikt antall masker	Odd number of stitches
Ull	Wool
Ull garn	Wool yarn
Under	Under

Underarm	Underarm
Unse	Ounce
Utelate	Miss; omit
Uten	Without
Utringning	Neckline
Vannrett	Horizontal
Vante	Glove
Venstre forstykke	Left front
Verk	Work
Vertikal	Vertical
Vest	Vest
Venstre pinne	Left needle
Veve	Weave
Veving	Weaving
Vidde	Width
Vr. bord 1 r., 1 vr.	K1, p1 rib
Vr. bord 2 r., 2 vr.	K2, p2 rib
Vrangbord	Rib; ribbing
Vrangbord strikking	Ribbed knitting

Vrangen	The wrong side (of work)
Vrangmaske	Purl stitch
Vrangomgang	Purl row
Vrangstrikking	Purl
Være igjen	Remain
5 strømpepinner	Set of 5 dp needles

FARGE	COLOR
Blå	Blue
Brun	Brown
Grå	Gray
Grønn	Green
Gul	Yellow
Hvit	White
Lilla	Purple
Lys	Light
Lyserød; rosa	Pink
Mørk	Dark
Naturfarget	Natural
Orange	Orange
Rød	Red
Svart	Black

Knitting in Spanish

SPANISH / ENGLISH

SPANISH	**ENGLISH**
A través	Through
Abrochar	Fasten
Acabar	Finish
Aguja(s)	Needles
Aguja auxiliar	Cable needle
Aguja circular	Circular needle
Aguja de punto	Knitting needle
Aguja de repuesto	Stitch holder or cable needle
Aguja derecha	Right needle
Aguja izquierda	Left needle
Aguja sujeta puntos	Stitch holder
Alternativamente	Alternate(ly)
Alto	Length
Alto total	Total length
Anillo	Loop
Antes	Before
Armado	Making up

Arrollado	Yarn forward, yarn over needle
Aumentar	To increase
Aumentos	Increases
Aún	Still
A cado extremo	At each end
Bolsillo	Pocket
Borde	Edge; border; selvedge
Borde anudato	Beaded selvedge
Borde cadeneta	Chain selvedge
Botón	Button
Bucle	Loop
Cadeneta	Chain
Calado	Lacy; slot for ribbon
Cambiar	To change
Canesú	Yoke
Centro, central	Center
Cerrar en redondo	Join into a ring
Cerrar	Cast off
Clave	Key (to chart)

Color	Color
Con	With
Continuar	Continue
Coser	To sew
Crecido (hacer un)	Yarn forward, yarn around the needle, yarn over
Cruzar	Cross (cable)
Cuello	Collar
Dar vuelta (labor)	To turn (the work)
De (en) una sola vez	In one row, in one time
Debajo	Under
Dejar en espera	Leave unworked
Delantero	Front
Derecha	On the right
Derecho	Right
Derecho del trabajo	Front or right side of work
Derecho de la labor	Right side of work
Deslizar uno o varios bucles	To draw through one or more loops

Después	After
Deslizar	Slip
Detrás	Through back of loop
Disminuir	Decrease
Dividir	To divide
Dobladillo	Hem
Doble	Double
Doble hebra	Double yarn
Echar (el hilo)	Take yarn round needle or hook
Elástico 1 X 1	K1, p1 rib
Elástico 2 X 2	K2, p2 rib
Empezar	Begin
En espera o dejar en suspenso	Leave stitches on stitch holder
Escote	Neck; neckline
Espalda	Back
Fino	Fine
Fruncir	Gather
Ganchillo	Crochet or crochet hook

104

Grueso	Thick
Hacer punto o tejer	To knit
Hebra	Yarn; yarn over needle; yarn forward
Hebra delante o atrás	Back or front loop (of stitch)
Hombro(s)	Shoulder(s)
Igual	Equal; the same
Impar	Odd (rows)
Invertir la explicación en sentido inverso	Reversing shaping or instructions
Izquierdo	Left (opposite to right)
Juego de agujas	Double-pointed needles
Juntos	Together (stitches)
Labor	Work
Lado	Side; edge
Largo	Length
Levantar	Pick up
Levantar puntos perdidos	To pick up dropped stitches
Levantar sin tejer	To slip

Manga	Sleeve
Marcha de la labor	Instructions
Media presilla	Half-treble (Amer:half double) crochet
Medidas	Measurements
Menguados o disminuyendo puntos	Decrease
Menguar	To decrease
Mitad	Half
Montaje	Casting on
Montar	To cast on
Muestra de orientación	Tension
Número de puntos múltiplo de X más X	Number of stitches divisible by X plus X
Ochos	Cables
Ojal	Buttonhole
Orillo	Selvedge
Ovillo	Ball
Par	Even (rows)
Parar	Fasten off
Pasada	Row

Pasada precedente	Previous row
Pasar el deslizado sobre el punto al derecho	Slip one, knit one, pass slipped stitch over
Pasar el deslizado sobre los dos puntos al derecho	Slip one, knit 2 together, pass slipped stitch over
Planchar	To iron, press
Presilla sencilla	Treble (Amer:double) crochet
Presilla doble	Double-treble (Amer: treble) crochet
Proceder igual	Work in the same way
Proseguir	Continue
Puño	Cuff
Punto	Stitch
Punto bobo	Garter stitch
Punto de arroz	Moss stitch
Punto cadeneta	Chain
Punto cruzado	Crossed stitch
Punto de cabeza	Top of stitch (crochet)
Punto de jersey	Stocking stitch
Punto de jersey revés	Reverse stocking stitch

Punto de malla	Knitting
Punto derecho	Knit stitch
Punto deslizado	Slip stitch
Puntos empleados	Stitches used
Punto en el aire	Chain
Punto fantasía	Patterns for which instructions are given separately
Punto levantado a la derecha	Slip stitch as if to knit
Punto levantado al revés	Slip stitch as if to purl
Punto musgo	Garter stitch
Punto orillo	Selvedge stitch
Punto prieto	Double (Amer: single) crochet
Punto rematado	Stitch passed over
Punto revés	Purl stitch
Punto torcido	Twisted or crossed stitches
Puntos	Together (stitches)
Raglán	Raglan
Recto	Straight, without shaping

108

Remallar	To pick up the loops
Repetir de * a *	Repeat from * to *
Restante	Remaining
Revés	Wrong side of work
Sacar un bucle	Draw through a loop
Saltar	Miss (Amer:skip) a stitch
Seguir	Continue
Siempre	Always
Siguiente	Following; next
Simultáneamente	At the same time
Sin	Without
Sisa	Armhole
Soltar un punto	To drop one stitch
Talla	Size
Tejer	To knit
Tejer en redondo	To knit in rounds
Tejer los puntos tal como se presentan	Knit the knit stitches and purl the purl stitches
Terminación	Casting off or binding off
Terminar	Finish

Tira	Strip; border
Todo	All; every
Trabajar	Work
Trenza	Cable
Unir	To join
Veces	Times
Volver	To work back (a stitch)
Volver a coger	Repeat from
Vuelta	Row (or round if on four needles)

COLOR

Amarilla	Yellow
Naranja	Orange
Azul	Blue
Blanca	White
Gris	Gray
Marrón; morena	Brown
Negra	Black
Purpúreo	Purple
Roja	Red
Rosa; rosada; de rosa	Pink
Verde	Green
Violeta	Purple

111

Knitting in Swedish

SWEDISH / ENGLISH

SWEDISH (SVENSK)*	ENGLISH
Akta sig	Take care
Allt	All
Alltid	Always
Antal maskar	Number of stitches
Antal varv på längden	Number of rows in length
Andra	Second
Arbeta jämnt	Work even
Arbeta tillbaka	Work back
Arbete	Work (knitting)
Av arbetet	Wrong side (of work)
Avig maska	Purl stitch
Avig slätstickning	Reverse stocking stitch
Aviga maskor	Purl stitch
Avigsida; avigsidan	Wrong side (of work)
Avigvarv	Purl row

PLEASE NOTE: Swedish words beginning with the letter "Å" or "Ä" are listed at the end of the alphabet.

Avmaska	Bind off; cast off; to bind off or cast off
Avmaska i mönster	Cast off in pattern
Avmaskad maska	Stitch passed over
Avmaskning	Casting off/binding off
Avvikande färg	Contrasting color (not used in pattern, but as a temporary stitch holding yarn to be later removed, such as for thumb in mittens or for pocket opening)
Axel	Shoulder
Axelsömmen	Shoulder seams
Bakifrån	Back loop (of st); through back of loop
Bakifrån (tagen)	Into back of stitch
Bakom	Behind
Bakre	Back of stitch
Bakstycke	Back
Basmodell	Basic model
Behandling av yllevaror	Care of (woolen articles)
Beskrivning	Instruction

Bomull	Cotton
Bystvidd	Chest measurement
Byt till	Change to
Både	Both sides of stitch
Bålen	Body
Bård	Border; front borders
Börja	Begin
Börja om	Start over
Början	Beginning
Cardigan	Cardigan
Del	Part
Dela i mitten	Divide at the center
Dra genom öglan (öglarna)	Draw through a loop; to draw through one or more loops
Dubbel överdragshoptagning	Slip one, knit two together pass slipped stitch over (sk2togp)
Dubbelstolpe	Double treble
Då	Then
Efterstygn	Backstitch

115

Knitting in Swedish
Swedish / English

Eller	Or
En storlek	One size
Endast	Only
Enligt	Following
Extra stor	Extra large
Fastmaska	Single or double crochet
Ficka	Pocket
Flotteringar	Floats (stranded yarn as seen from the wrong side)
Fläta	Cable
Forma	Shape
Forma halsen	Neck shaping
Forma ärmen	Sleeve shaping
Framifrån	Through front of loop
Framifrån maskbåge	Front loop (of st)
Framkant	Front band
Framstycke	Front
Främre	Front of stitch
Fålla	Hem

Fånga upp (tappade maskor)	Pick up (dropped sts)
Fånga tappade maskor	To pick up dropped sts
Från * till *	From * to *
Färg	Color
Färgställning	Color combination
Fäst alla trådar	Fasten off
Följa	Follow
Föregående	Previous
Förklaring	Explanation
Försedd med pärlor	Beaded
Först	First
Garn	Yarn
Garnboll	Pompom
Garner	Yarns
Gram	Grams
Grovlek	Needle size
Grovt garn	Thick yarn
Gånger	Times
Gör	Make

Halsduk	Scarf
Halsen	Neckline
Halskant	Neckband; neck binding (i.e., crew neck or V-neck)
Halslinning	Neckband - inner
Halsringningen	Neckline
Halvstolpe	Half double crochet
Handske	Glove
Hela längden	Complete length
Hjälpsticka	Cable needle; stitch holder
Hoppa över	Skip over
Hoptagning	Decreasing
Hålmönster	Eyelet pattern
Härva	Skein (hank)
Höger	Right (as opposed to left)
Höger framstycke	Right front; right side
Höger hand	Right hand
Höger sida	Right side (of work) (as opposed to the left side of the work)

I bakre maskbågen	Into back of stitch
I ett stycke	In one piece
I färg	In color
Intagning	Decreasing
Jacka	Cardigan
Jumper	Pullover sweater
Jumpersticka	Straight needles
Jämna varv	Even number row
Jämntfördelade	Evenly spaced
Kant	Edge; selvedge
Kantmaska	Edge stitch; selvedge stitch
Kastad	Yarn over
Kedjemaska	Chain (for crochet)
Kedjesömkant	Chain selvedge
Kil	Gusset (underarm)
Kjol	Skirt
Knapp	Button
Knappar	Buttons
Knapphål	Buttonhole

Knapphålsslå	Buttonhole band
Knappslå	Button band
Kofta	Cardigan
Korsa	Cross a stitch; to cross
Korsstyng	Cross stitch (embroidery)
Kort	Short
Krage	Collar
Liten	Small
Lodräta	Vertical
Luftmaska	Chain (for crochet); slip stitch
Lyft	Skip (a stitch)
Lyfta	Slip a stitch; to slip
Lyftad avig maska	Slip stitch as if to purl
Lyftad rät maska	Slip stitch as if to knit
Lång	Long
Lägg upp	Cast on
Lägga	To place
Lämna på (avmaskningsnål)	Leave sts on st holder

120

Lämna på (hjälpsticka)	Leave sts on cable needle
Lämna kvar	Leave remaining
Längd	Length
Manschett(er)	Cuff(s)
Maska	Stitch
Maska av	To cast off or bind off
Maska av maskarna	Cast off all stitches
Maskatäthet	Tension
Maskbågen	Top of stitch (crochet)
Maskhållare	Stitch holder
Masktäthet	Gauge
Med garnet bak	Yarn back
Med garnet fram	Yarn forward
Med stickor, sticka	Knit
Medium	Medium
Minska	Decrease a number of sts; to decrease
Minskningar	Decrease
Missa	Miss
Mitt-; medel-; mellerst-	Middle

Mittmaskan	Central stitch
Montera	Sew together
Montering	Finishing; to make up
Mosstickning	Moss stitch
Mosstickning (k1, p1)	Seed stitch
Muscher	Bobble pattern
Mått	Measurement
Mäta	Measure
Mössa	Cap
Mönster	Pattern stitch
Nummer	Number
Nystan	Ball
Nästa	Second
Ok	Yoke
Ollekrage	Turtle neck
Omlott	Over each other
Omslag	Yarn around needle; yarn over
Omslag, AM	Yarn over needle before purl stitch

Omslag, RM	Yarn over needle before knit stitch
Ögla	Loop
Öka	To increase
Ökningar	Increase
Öppning	Opening
Överallt i	Through
Överdragshoptagning (öhpt)	Slip one, knit one, pass slipped stitch over (skp) or K2 together
Övervidd	Width
Passande	Suitable
Placera	To place
Plagg	Article (of clothing)
Plattstickning	Flat knitting (w/2 ndls)
Plocka upp	To knit up or pick up
Plocka upp (en maska)	Knit up or pick up stitches
Plocka upp (maskar)	To pick up loops or sts
Plocka upp och sticka	Pick up and knit
Pressa	Press
Provlapp	Swatch (for gauge)

Pullover	Vest (without buttons - pullover vest)
På en gång	At the same time
På höger sidan	On the right
På längden	Lengthwise
På samma sätt	Alike; similarly
På vänster sidan	On the left
Påarbete	Front or right side of work
Pärlkant	Seam edge
Rand	Stripe
Randig	Striped
Rapport	Repeat (as in pattern repeat)
Rapport på (X + X)	Work on a multiple of X plus X stitches
Ren ull	Wool on the ball
Repa upp	Unravel
Resår	Rib; ribbed knitting
Resår *1 rm, 1 am*	K1, p1 rib
Resår *2 rm, 2 am*	K2, p2 rib
Resårstickning	Ribbed knitting

Ribbstickning	Ribbed knitting
Rundst	Circular needle
Rundsticka	Circular needle
Rundstickning	Circular or round knitting
Ränder	Stripes
Rät maska	Knit stitch
Rätmaska	Plain knitting
Rätsida	Right side (of work) (the side that shows)
Rätstickning	Garter stitch
Rätt	Right (as opposed to wrong)
Rättsidan på arbetet	Front or right side of work
Rättsticka	Right needle
Rättvarv	Knit row
Samma	Same
Samtidigt	At the same time
Separat	Separate
Sicksack	Zigzag
Sicksackrörelse	Zigzag movement
Sida	Side

Swedish	English
Silke; silkesgarn	Silk
Sist	Last
Sjal	Shawl
Sjalkrage	Shawl color
Skarva	Join
Slå knut på	Tie a knot
Slätstickning	Knit plain (knit); stockinette or stocking stitch
Smygmaska	Slip stitch
Sno [snor, snos]	Strand
Snodd maska	Twisted or crossed stitch
Som om	As if
Spets	Lace
Spänna; sträcka	Stretch (the pieces for blocking)
Sticka	Knitting needle; to knit
Sticka avigt	Purl
Sticka ihop	Knit together
Sticka som	Work as for

Stickas som (höger, vänster) men åt motsatt hål	Reverse the instructions
Stickas som (höger, vänster) men åt motsatt hål	Reverse shapings
Stickbeskrivning	Knitting instructions
Stickfasthet	Gauge
Stickerskor	Knitters
Stickning	Knitting
Stickpaket	Kits
Stolpe	Treble
Stor	Large
Storlek	Size
Ställa	To place
Strumpst	Set of 5 dp needles
Strumpsticka	Double-pointed needle
Strumpstickor	Double-pointed needles
Sträckning	Stretch (how much a knitted fabric does)
Strycka	Iron
Stycke	Part

127

Summa	Total
Sy	Sew
Sy sömmen	Sew seams
Sätta	To place
Sätt på avmaskningsnål	Place on stitch holder
Sätt på hjälpsticka	Place on cable needle
Sätt på maskhållare	Place on stitch holder
Söm	Seam
Sömkant	Seam edge
Sömsmån	Seam allowance
Ta upp	Knit up or pick up stitches
Tag av garnet	Break the yarn
Tappa en maska	Drop a stitch; to drop a stitch
Till höger	On the right
Till vänster	On the left
Tillsammans	Together (sts)
Tofs	Tassle
Total	Total
Totalt	Altogether

128

Tröja	Pullover sweater; sweater
Tumkil	Thumb shaping (in mittens)
Tunnt garn	Thin yarn
Udda maskantal	Odd number of stitches
Udda varv	Odd number row
Ull	Wool (in its natural state)
Under	Under
Underärmen	Underarm
Uns (= 28.4 grams)	Ounce
Uppläggning	Casting on
Upprepa	To repeat
Upprepa dessa X varv	Repeat these X rows
Upprepa från *	Repeat from *
Upprepade	Repeated
Utan; utanför	Without
Valkning	Boiled wool (felting)
Var	Each
Var och en	Each
Vara kvar	Remain

Knitting in Swedish
Swedish / English

Swedish	English
Varannan; vartannat varv	Every other
Varje	Each; every
Varv	Round; row
Varvantal	Number of rows
Vik in	Fold in
Virka	Crochet
Virka kant; virkad kant	Crochet border
Virknål	Crochet hook
Vriden	Knit into back of stitch
Vriden maska	Twisted or crossed stitch
Vågrätt	Horizontal
Vända	To turn (the work)
Vänster framsida	Left front
Vänster sticka	Left needle
Väst	Vest (with button front)
Vävning	Weaving
Växelvis	Alternately
Växla	Change
Ylle	Wool yarn

Ylle strumpor	Wool socks/stockings
Ylletyg	Wool cloth
Åt motsatt hål	Reverse
Återstående	Remainder
Ärm	Sleeve
Ärmhål	Armhole
Ärmkil	Underarm
Ärmkupan	Sleeve cap
Även	Also

Knitting in Swedish
Swedish / English

FARG

FARG	**COLOR**
Blek, ljus	Light
Blått	Blue
Brunt	Brown
Grått	Grey
Grönt	Green
Gult	Yellow
Lila	Purple
Mörkt	Dark
Naturvit; naturgrå; natursvart	Natural
Orange	Orange
Rosa	Pink
Rött	Red
Svart	Black
Vitt	White